Seeing the STARS

John and Mary Gribbin

OXFORD
UNIVERSITY PRESS

OXFORD
UNIVERSITY PRESS

is a department of the University of Oxford.
It furthers the University's objective of excellence in research, scholarship,
and education by publishing worldwide in

Oxford   New York

Auckland   Cape Town   Dar es Salaam   Hong Kong   Karachi
Kuala Lumpur   Madrid   Melbourne   Mexico City   Nairobi
New Delhi   Shanghai   Taipei   Toronto

With offices in

Argentina   Austria   Brazil   Chile   Czech Republic   France   Greece
Guatemala   Hungary   Italy   Japan   Poland   Portugal   Singapore
South Korea   Switzerland   Thailand   Turkey   Ukraine   Vietnam

Oxford is a registered trade mark of Oxford University Press
in the UK and in certain other countries

British Library Cataloguing in Publication Data

Data available

ISBN: 978-0-19-846108-1

1 3 5 7 9 10 8 6 4 2

Printed in China

Paper used in the production of this book is a natural,
recyclable product made from wood grown in sustainable forests.
The manufacturing process conforms to the environmental
regulations of the country of origin

Acknowledgements

The publisher would like to thank the following for permission to reproduce photographs: **p7**r Phototake
Inc./Alamy; **p8** David Parker/Science Photo Library; **p9**bl Sandy Huffaker/Stringer/Getty Images, **p9**br Dr
Seth Shostak/Science Photo Library, **p9**t TopFoto; **p10** SPL/Mark Garlick; **p11**tl Dr Rudolph Schild/Science
Photo Library, **p11**tr&b The Hubble Heritage Team/STScl/AURA/NASA; **p12** Matthias Kulka/Zefa/Corbis
UK Ltd.; **p13**t Corbis UK Ltd., **p13**c Rex Features, **p13**b Pictor International/ImageState/Alamy; **p14**l
Cosmo Condina/Alamy, **p14**r Jon Arnold Images/Alamy; **p16**l NASA Headquarters - Greatest Images of
NASA (NASA-HQ-GRIN)/NASA, **p16**r NASA; **p17**tl&tr NASA Jet Propulsion Laboratory (NASA-JPL)/NASA,
p17bl J.P.Harrington/K.J.Borkowski/University of Maryland/NASA, **p17**br ESA/Hubble Heritage Team
(STScI/AURA)/NASA, **p17**c AURA/STScI/NASA; **p19**t Robin Scagell/Galaxy Picture Library, **p19**b Institute for
Computational Cosmology, Durham University, UK; **p20**t Bettmann/Corbis UK Ltd., **p20**c AP Photo/Em-
pics, **p20**b NASA Jet Propulsion Laboratory (NASA-JPL)/NASA; **p21** NMPFT Daily Herald Archive/Science &
Society Picture Library; **p22**l&r NASA Jet Propulsion Laboratory (NASA-JPL)/NASA; **p23**b NASA

Cover: Corbis/©1989 Roger Ressmeyer with Ian Shelton

Illustrations by Peter Bull Art Studio: **p4**, **p5**, **p6**, **p7**, **p15**, **p18**l , **p21**; Andy Parker: **p18**r, **p23**

Contents

Galileo's telescope

Almost four hundred years ago, an Italian called Galileo Galilei heard about a new invention. It was a hollow tube with a lens at each end, like the lenses in eyeglasses, and it magnified things and made distant objects look closer. Galileo had never seen a telescope, but when he heard the news he made one himself. It was the best telescope anyone had ever made. He looked through it at the night sky and made many discoveries.

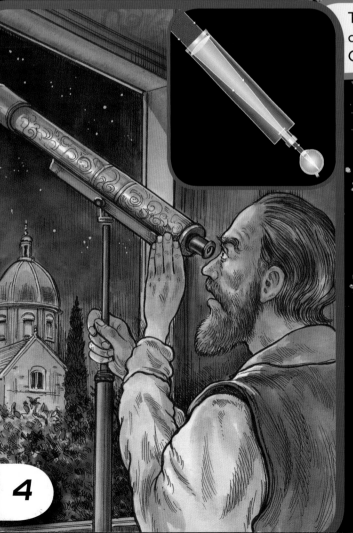

This is a cross-section of the sort of telescope Galileo used

A telescope doesn't just magnify things. Because the opening of a telescope is bigger than the opening in your eye (the pupil), it gathers more light and makes faint objects look brighter.

Before they had telescopes, astronomers thought that the **stars** were little points of light quite close to us. They looked for patterns in the stars, called constellations, but they didn't know the difference between stars and **planets.**

Galileo saw that, through a telescope, the planets look like discs in the sky. They are close to us and **orbit** round the Sun.

Galileo discovered that he could see **moons** orbiting around the planet Jupiter, and he saw that the band of light across the sky, called the **Milky Way**, is made up of millions and millions of stars.

Jupiter and three of its largest moons

FACT

Stars look like tiny points of light, even through a telescope. But they are really big, hot objects like the Sun. They look small only because they are very far away.

The Solar System

Astronomy only began to be scientific after telescopes were invented. Telescopes helped astronomers to see that, just as the moons go round Jupiter, the planets go round the Sun.

The Sun is a star about a hundred times wider than our Earth, but it doesn't look that big because it is 149 million kilometres away from us. All the planets that go round the Sun, including Earth, are part of the Solar System.

The Sun shines because it is very hot, like a furnace. Planets are not hot enough to shine, and we can see them only because they reflect the light from the Sun.

The sun with an imaginary chain of earths across it.

WARNING

You must never look at the Sun. It is so bright you could damage your eyesight permanently by staring at it even for a second.

The four planets closest to the Sun – Mercury, Venus, Earth and Mars – are all made of rock. The four planets beyond Mars – Jupiter, Saturn, Uranus and Neptune – are all made of gas, and they are very big, so they are called gas giants. Beyond Neptune is a tiny, icy object smaller than our Moon, called Pluto, which was once considered to be a planet.

The nearest star to the Sun is more than forty million million kilometres away. It takes light more than four years to travel from this star, called Proxima, to us. So it is more than four light years away.

Light year:
The distance light can travel in a year is called a light year. It is 9.46 million million kilometres. A light year is a measurement of distance, not time.

Astronomical mountaineers

To see very faint objects you need very big telescopes. Galileo's telescope was small enough for him to be able to carry around, but modern astronomers use huge telescopes housed in special buildings called observatories. Astronomers want to get the best view of the sky they can, so they build observatories on mountain tops, high above the clouds.

The William Herschel Telescope at La Palma, Canary Islands, built high above the clouds

FACT

All the artificial light in towns and cities dazzles telescopes, so this is another reason for building observatories on mountain tops – where there's no artificial light!

One of the first mountain-top observatories was built on Mount Wilson in California, USA, nearly a hundred years ago. There were no roads up the mountain, so all the material for the observatory had to be carried up on the backs of mules. The mirror for the big telescope there is 2.5 metres across.

Astronomers today don't often look through their telescopes. Instead, the light from the telescopes is focused on sensitive detectors connected to computers. Astronomers study the images and information on computer screens.

Galaxies — islands in space

The big telescopes show us that the Milky Way is made up of hundreds of billions of stars spread out in a disc with a bulge in the middle, shaped rather like a fried egg. But this 'fried egg' is so big that light takes more than a hundred thousand years to get from one side of it to the other. It is more than a hundred thousand light years across. Our Solar System is two-thirds of the way out from the centre of the disc.

Solar System

Outer

Perseus

Carina-Sagittarius

Crux-Scutum

Norma

As well as planets and stars, small telescopes also show us fuzzy blobs of light in the sky; but with big telescopes, astronomers can see that these blobs are made of billions and billions of stars. They are like islands in space, millions of light years away. These islands of stars are called galaxies, and just as our Sun is an ordinary star, our Milky Way is an ordinary **galaxy**. Because it is the galaxy we live in, we call it the Galaxy, with a capital G.

FACT

A typical galaxy contains about 100 billion stars and it would take around 100,000 light years to cross from one side of the galaxy to the other.

Seeing invisible light

Our eyes can see all the colours of the rainbow – red, orange, yellow, green, blue, indigo and violet. But there are 'colours' that our eyes cannot see: redder than red and more violet than violet. These invisible colours are called infrared and ultraviolet. Special kinds of telescopes can 'see' these colours. Astronomers can learn more about the stars, planets and galaxies using infrared and ultraviolet light to look at them.

Invisible light can be focused on to special photographic film, which produces pictures we can see. It can also be focused on to chips like the ones in a digital camera, so that computers can turn the invisible images into ones we can see.

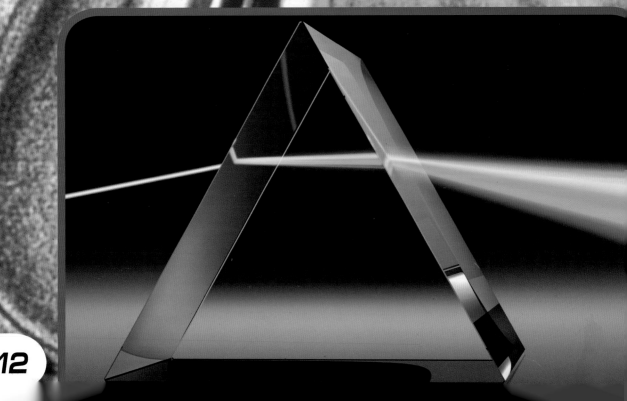

Some infrared telescopes can work from mountain tops. However, most of the invisible light from space is blocked by the Earth's atmosphere and never reaches the ground, so the telescopes have to be flown into space to measure this light

'SAF MARK IVB

This image from a weather satellite shows the 'Northern Lights' as well as light from the cities of northern Europe

Spectrum:
The name for all the colours of the rainbow is a spectrum.

FACT

The atmosphere is the layer of gases surrounding a planet.

Radio ears and X-ray vision

Radio waves are also a kind of invisible light, but radio waves do travel through the atmosphere. Astronomers build huge radio antennae to 'listen' to the radio waves from objects in space. The waves don't sound like radio programmes. They are just a kind of noise, like the hissing you can hear when a radio isn't tuned properly.

These dishes make up the world's largest radio telescope, in New Mexico, USA. It is known as The Very Large Array

X-rays are a very powerful kind of invisible light. They come from energetic stars in space. Living things on Earth aren't damaged by the radiation from X-ray light because the atmosphere surrounding the Earth stops the X-rays from getting through.

Special telescopes on satellites study the X-rays. The data from the satellites is radioed down to astronomers on the ground.

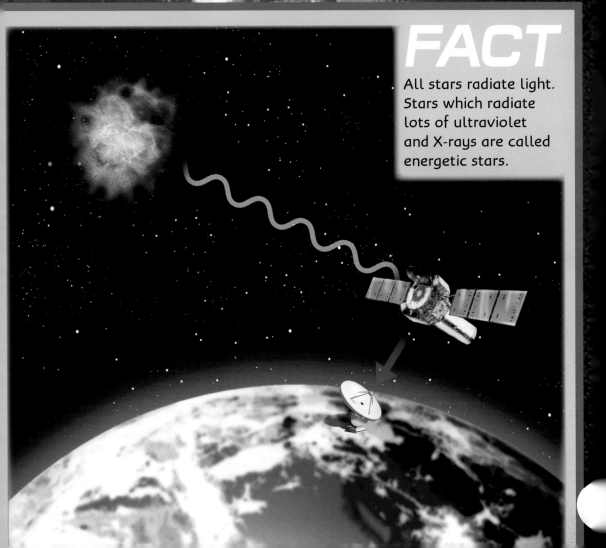

FACT

All stars radiate light. Stars which radiate lots of ultraviolet and X-rays are called energetic stars.

The Hubble Space Telescope

The most famous telescope flies in space, but it uses ordinary light to get images of stars and galaxies. It is called the Hubble Space Telescope (HST) and was launched in 1990. The mirror on the HST is as big as the mirror on the big telescope at Mount Wilson, USA. It's like a mountain-top observatory flying through space.

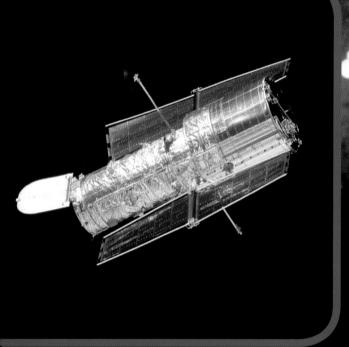

The HST is getting quite old for a space observatory. But it is still doing good work because visiting astronauts have upgraded its instruments. They have also repaired broken instruments

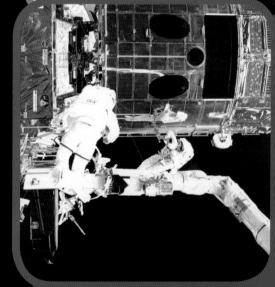

The Hubble Space Telescope orbits outside the Earth's atmosphere and can send back images of objects in space that are billions of light years away.

Photos from the Hubble

Saturn with its rings

The Crab Nebula

The Tarantula Nebula

The Cat's Eye Nebula

The Eagle Nebula

Computer wizards

Today's astronomers lead very different lives from those of Galileo's time. They travel the world to visit observatories on mountains, in places like Hawaii and Chile. Even when they use telescopes in space, they have to travel to places like Japan and the United States to work at the ground stations where information from space telescopes is received.

Computer linkups enable astronomers to work almost anywhere. By using the Internet they can almost instantly share information and discoveries with other astronomers all over the world.

Ground station:
A place on Earth where scientists send instructions to satellites and get back data is called a ground station.

Astronomy is the most international of all the sciences

Astronomy isn't just about taking fantastic pictures. Astronomers also need to be computer wizards. They use some of the biggest computers in the world to analyse the data they get from their telescopes. That's how they find out about things like energetic stars.

Supercomputer COSMA-3

FACT

- Each of the Earth's 6 billion people would need to complete 166,666 calculations per second to keep up with a supercomputer.
- A supercomputer can process information equivalent to 20 million books in less than 30 seconds.

19

Astronomical superstars

Cecilia Payne-Gaposchkin

Cecilia Payne was born in England in 1900. She went to Cambridge University and then worked at the Harvard Observatory, USA. She married another astronomer, Sergei Gaposchkin, and added his surname to hers. She was the first person to work out what stars are made of.

Clyde Tombaugh

Clyde Tombaugh was born in 1906. He was too poor to go to university, but he built his own telescope and loved looking at stars. When he was 29 he got a job at the Lowell Observatory in Arizona, USA. A year later, he discovered Pluto, which was then thought of as a planet.

FACT

Pluto is a tiny, icy object smaller than our Moon, at the edge of the Solar System. Most astronomers now think it is not big enough to be called a planet.

Milton Humason

Milton Humason was born in 1893. He left school when he was 14 and worked on Mount Wilson, California, USA, with the mule trains, taking the bits for the 250 centimetre telescope up the mountain. He loved the mountain so much that he got a job as a janitor at the observatory and worked his way up to become an astronomer.

Jocelyn Bell

Jocelyn Bell was born in Belfast in 1943. She went to the University of Cambridge and studied radio astronomy. While she was still a student, in 1967, she discovered a new kind of radio star, called a pulsar. The 'telescope' she used to discover pulsars was a field covered in wires.

FACT

A pulsar is a tiny star that spins very fast – up to a thousand times every second. Each time a pulsar spins it sends out 'pulses' of radio noise that can be picked up by radio telescopes.

Other 'Earths'

Modern telescopes show us that there are lots of other stars with planets going round them, like our Solar System. Because big planets are easier to find than small planets, most of the planets discovered so far are big, like Jupiter. But astronomers think that there must be lots of smaller planets like Earth still to be found.

A set of space telescopes, called the Terrestrial Planet Finder, is being developed. The Terrestrial Planet Finder will be big enough to see other Earth-like planets, and might be launched by the year 2020.

This is an artist's concept of what a planet circling a distant star would look like viewed through infared light

There doesn't seem to be any life on the other planets in our Solar System, only on Earth. But if other 'Earths' exist in other solar systems, there might be living beings on those planets looking at our Solar System through their telescopes. Perhaps on another planet orbiting around a star thousands of light years away, a being like Galileo is just inventing a telescope!

Several unmanned space probes have landed on Mars and carried out experiments. Astronomers studied all the information that the space probes sent back but they could not find any sign of any kind of life on the planet.

Mini Quiz

1. Who discovered the moons of Jupiter?
2. How long does it take light to cross the Milky Way galaxy?
3. Who was a mule train driver before becoming an astronomer?
4. Why do astronomers build observatories on mountain tops?
5. How many stars are there in a galaxy?

Glossary

galaxy – an island of stars in space
Milky Way – the name of the galaxy we live in
moon – a cold lump of ice or rock that orbits a planet
orbit – the path followed by a planet going round a star, or by a moon going round a planet
planet – a cool ball of rock or gas that orbits a star. The Earth is a planet
star – a hot fireball of gas much bigger than a planet. The Sun is a star

Index

1. Galileo Galilei
2. More than a hundred thousand years
3. Milton Humason
4. To get the best view of the sky and to stop artificial light dazzling their telescopes
5. About 100 billion stars